The Art of Good Food

POTATO FILLINGS

The Art of Good Food

POTATO FILLINGS

JON HIGGINS

Illustrated by
PAUL COLLICUT

COOMBE BOOKS

The Art of Good Food
POTATO FILLINGS
Designed and created by
THE BRIDGEWATER BOOK COMPANY LTD

Designer Sarah Stanley
Editor Donna Wood
Managing Editor Anna Clarkson
Illustrations Paul Collicut
Page make-up Martyn Feather

CLB 4588
This edition published 1996 by Coombe Books
© 1995 CLB PUBLISHING
Godalming, Surrey
All rights reserved.
Origination by Sussex Repro Ltd England
Printed and bound in Singapore by Tien Wah Press
ISBN 1-85833-495-0

Contents

▍Introduction *10*

MEAT AND POULTRY

▍Spice-dusted Beef with Coconut Sauce *12*
▍Creamy Bacon & Mushrooms *14*
▍Honey-glazed Chicken Bites *15*
▍Spicy Tomato & Chorizo Sausage *17*
▍Ham & Broccoli Stuffed Potatoes *18*
▍Savoury Mince *19*
▍Easy Chilli *19*
▍Sausage, Egg & Bacon Jackets *20*
▍Grilled Chicken with Garlic Butter *22*
▍Chinese Beef & Green Pepper *23*
▍Italian Ham & Cheese *25*
▍Crunchy Chicken *26*
▍Cheese & Bacon *26*
▍Mini Saté & Peanut Sauce *27*
▍Fragrant Lamb in Rosemary Gravy *28*
▍Barbecued Belly of Pork *31*
▍Chicken & Apricot Curry *32*
▍Broad Beans & Bacon *33*
▍Calves Liver with Sweet Red Onions *34*

FISH

▍Smoked Haddock & Tomato *36*
▍Prawn & Avocado *38*
▍Scrambled Eggs & Smoked Salmon *39*
▍Piquant Flaked Salmon *39*
▍Fresh Steamed Mussels with Parsley *41*
▍Kipper & Egg Mash *42*
▍King Prawns in Lime & Dill Mayonnaise *43*
▍Tuna with Multi-coloured Peppers *45*
▍Sardine & Tomato Hash *46*
▍Rolled Fresh Anchovies *46*
▍Seafood & Tomato *48*
▍Tangy Crab & Prawn *48*
▍Calamari in Spinach & Cream Sauce *51*
▍Deep-fried Devilled Whitebait *52*

VEGETARIAN

▍Mixed Bean Salad Jackets *54*
▍Welsh Tatties *56*
▍Spicy Vegetable Curry *57*
▍Spicy Guacamole Potatoes *59*
▍Curried Potato & Egg Jackets *60*
▍Ratatouille Topping *61*
▍Red Cabbage with Cashew Nuts *62*
▍Spinach & Cream Cheese Soufflé *64*
▍Crunchy Blue Cheese & Walnut *65*
▍Sultana Cauliflower Cheese *67*
▍Chick Pea Curry *68*
▍Coleslaw & Bavarian Cheese *68*

▍Grilled Goats' Cheese with Basil *69*
▍Garlicky Mushroom & Hazelnuts *70*
▍Home-made Herb Mayonnaise *72*
▍Deep-fried Potato Skins with Salad *73*
▍Carrot & Broad Bean Puffs *75*

▍Index *76*

Introduction

The humble potato is part of everyone's diet; in one form or another we eat this most versatile of vegetables at least once a day. We boil, mash and chip away week in, week out, without actually thinking about its other possibilities. Yet what could be simpler than scrubbing the skins and placing the potatoes in a preheated oven for an hour or so, or if you lead a hectic lifestyle, microwaving for a mere ten minutes?

Of course, cooking the potato is only the beginning. There is an almost endless variety of fillings that can be used to bring excitement to meal times, from the rich and exotic sauces ideal for candlelit suppers, to the quick and healthy fillings for those on the move, but who need to watch their waistline.

The collection of recipes contained in this book has been chosen to appeal to the widest range of tastes, from young to old, palates that vary from the straightforward to the sophisticated and from quickly prepared dishes to those that are a little more involved. There is also a section especially for vegetarians.

CHOOSING POTATOES FOR BAKING

Choose potatoes of roughly similar size, approximately 225g–275g (8–10oz) in weight is ideal. Because potatoes are a product of Mother Nature they do not grow to identical shapes and sizes, so pick carefully and avoid any that are scuffed or green, or have deep eyes which can make cleaning difficult. Also avoid any potatoes that have excess soil adhering to them; this is tedious to remove and as potatoes are usually sold by weight you will end up paying for soil! Almost all varieties of old potatoes (also known as maincrop potatoes) are suitable for baking, but Maris Piper, King Edward, Desirée and Cara are particularly good. At one time it would have been impossible to tell one type from another unless you had extensive knowledge of potatoes, but a legal obligation on retailers to show clearly variety names at sales points means you can now purchase the type you want.

STORING POTATOES

If necessary, remove the potatoes from their polythene packaging and store them unwashed in a dark, cool place that gets plenty of air. This will ensure that the potatoes stay in the peak of condition.

TO BAKE A POTATO IN A CONVENTIONAL OVEN

1   Preheat the oven to 220°C/425°F/Gas Mark 7.
2   Scrub the potatoes well under cold running water. Prick the skins all over with a fork to allow steam to escape during cooking and prevent the skins from bursting open. If desired, brush the skins with a little oil, this will give a glossy appearance to the surface of the potato when it is baked.
3   Put the potatoes directly on the oven shelf and leave to cook for 1–1¼ hours or until the potato feels soft when lightly squeezed. You can reduce cooking time a little by spearing the potatoes onto metal skewers.

TO BAKE A POTATO IN A MICROWAVE OVEN

1   Scrub the potatoes well under cold running water and prick the skins with a fork to prevent bursting.
2   Place the potatoes well apart in the microwave oven (650w) on a few sheets of absorbent kitchen paper, and cook on full power. Allow one potato about eight minutes cooking time, two potatoes about 15 minutes and four potatoes about 25 minutes.

Using a microwave oven is fine to bake potatoes if you are in a hurry, but they will never equal the delicious combination of crunchy skin and fluffy insides obtained by conventional cooking methods.

Meat and Poultry

Spice-dusted Beef with Coconut Sauce

SERVES 4

This exotic mix of flavours adds a touch of mystery to meal times

INGREDIENTS

4 large baking potatoes
450g/1lb sirloin steak
10ml/2 tsp garam masala
2.5ml/½tsp turmeric
vegetable oil
1 onion, finely chopped
12g/½oz fresh ginger, finely grated
50g/2oz fresh grated coconut
150ml/5fl oz double cream
salt and pepper

▌Begin by setting the potatoes to bake in a hot oven as recommended in the introduction.

▌Using a sharp knife slice the steak into thin strips and lay them out on a plate. Mix together the garam masala and turmeric and sprinkle the mixture evenly over the strips of steak, turning to ensure that they are well coated.

▌Heat 30ml/2tbsp of vegetable oil in a frying pan until smoking then add the steak a few strips at a time and quickly fry on both sides until nicely browned.

▌Remove the meat from the pan and place on some absorbent kitchen paper to soak up any excess oil.

▌When all the meat has been cooked, add a further 15ml/1tbsp oil to the pan and fry the chopped onion until nicely browned, add the fresh ginger and coconut to the pan and stir for a few minutes.

▌Lower the heat and add the double cream, stirring for a few minutes until all the flavours have combined and the sauce is hot.

▌Return the spicy beef to the pan and coat well in the sauce. Test a little on a teaspoon and correct the seasoning.

▌Cut the baked potatoes two-thirds of the way through and gently ease them open, fluff up the insides with a fork. Divide the topping between the potatoes and serve.

TIME: *Preparation takes about 10 minutes. Cooking takes approximately 15 minutes.*

Meat and Poultry

Creamy Bacon & Mushrooms

SERVES 4

Use plain or smoked bacon according to taste

INGREDIENTS

4 large baking potatoes
6 rashers smoked back bacon
50g/2oz butter
2 cloves garlic, crushed
6 spring onions, sliced
225g/8oz mushrooms, sliced
5ml/1 tsp cornflour
a little milk
pinch of grated nutmeg
200g/7oz tub full-fat fromage frais
salt and pepper

▌Begin by setting the potatoes to bake in a hot oven as recommended in the introduction.
▌Remove the rind from the bacon and discard. Cut the bacon into strips.
▌Melt the butter in a frying pan and sauté the bacon and garlic until the bacon begins to brown. Stir in the spring onions and mushrooms and sauté for 5–6 minutes or until the mushrooms are soft.
▌Mix the cornflour to a smooth paste with a little milk, then stir into the pan. Add the nutmeg, then stir in the fromage frais. Bring carefully to simmering point and simmer for 2 minutes; do not to let the mixture boil. Season to taste with salt, pepper and nutmeg.
▌When the potatoes are cooked, cut a cross in the top of each one. Gently squeeze each potato to open out the cross slightly.
▌Spoon the mushroom mixture on top and serve immediately.

TIME: *Preparation takes about 15 minutes. Cooking takes approximately 10 minutes.*
WATCHPOINT: *Do not use the very low-fat fromage frais in this recipe as it will curdle.*

Meat and Poultry

Honey-glazed Chicken Bites

SERVES 4

This is a very simple but delicious topping

INGREDIENTS

4 large baking potatoes

350g/12oz cooked warm chicken, skinned and cut into chunks

1 bunch of spring onions, roughly chopped

50g/2oz walnuts, roughly chopped

75ml/3fl oz clear honey

2.5ml/½ tsp cayenne pepper

salt and pepper

▌Begin by setting the potatoes to bake in a hot oven as recommended in the introduction.

▌In a large mixing bowl combine all the remaining ingredients and carefully mix together.

▌When cooked, cut a deep cross almost through the potatoes and allow them to fan out. Melt a little butter into each potato and spoon on the topping.

TIME: *Preparation takes about 10 minutes.*
SERVING IDEA: *This is delicious for lunch on a hot summer's day if served with a fresh green salad and a glass of chilled white wine.*

Meat and Poultry

Spicy Tomato & Chorizo Sausage
SERVES 4

A Mediterranean combination of spicy sausage and fresh tomatoes

INGREDIENTS
4 large baking potatoes
30ml/2 tbsp olive oil
1 Spanish onion, chopped
3 cloves garlic, crushed
5ml/1 tsp paprika
450g/1lb tomatoes, preferably plum, skinned and roughly chopped
150g/5oz chorizo or other spicy sausage, sliced

▌Begin by setting the potatoes to bake in a hot oven as recommended in the introduction.

▌Heat the oil in a saucepan and fry the onion until soft and beginning to brown.

▌Add the garlic and paprika and fry for a further 2 minutes.

▌Stir in the chopped tomatoes and bring gently to the boil.

▌Add the chorizo to the pan. Reduce the heat and simmer gently for 20–25 minutes.

▌When the potatoes are cooked, cut a cross in the top of each one. Gently squeeze each potato to open out the cross slightly.

▌Pile the sausage mixture on top and serve.

TIME: *Preparation takes about 10 minutes. Cooking takes approximately 30 minutes.*

Meat and Poultry

Ham & Broccoli Stuffed Potatoes

SERVES 4

A *great supper dish for all the family*

INGREDIENTS

4 large baking potatoes
225g/8oz broccoli florets
salt and pepper
25g/1oz butter
25g/1oz plain flour
300ml/10fl oz milk
pinch of grated nutmeg
50g/2oz sweetcorn kernels
175g/6oz ham, diced

▌Begin by setting the potatoes to bake in a hot oven as recommended in the introduction.
▌Blanch the broccoli in lightly salted boiling water for 5 minutes and drain well.
▌Melt the butter in a saucepan. Stir in the flour and cook over a low heat for 1 minute.
▌Gradually add the milk a little at a time until it has all been incorporated and you have a beautifully smooth sauce of coating consistency.
▌Season to taste with salt, pepper and nutmeg.
▌Add the blanched broccoli, the sweetcorn and ham, and heat through.
▌When the potatoes are cooked, cut in half and scoop out the flesh. Mash well.
▌Add the broccoli and ham mixture and mix gently until well combined.
▌Spoon back into the potato skins and serve.

TIME: *Preparation takes about 5 minutes. Cooking takes approximately 10 minutes.*
WATCHPOINT: *Take care not to overcook the broccoli at the beginning or it will disintegrate completely.*

Meat and Poultry

Savoury Mince

SERVES 4

The perfect accompaniment for baked potatoes

INGREDIENTS

4 large baking potatoes

30ml/2 tbsp sunflower oil

1 large onion, chopped

2 cloves garlic, crushed

350g/12oz lean minced pork

1 green pepper, seeded and chopped

125g/4oz mushrooms, sliced

400g/14oz can chopped tomatoes with herbs

30ml/2 tbsp tomato purée

50g/2oz butter

150ml/5fl oz double cream

chopped parsley to garnish

▎Begin by setting the potatoes to bake in a hot oven as recommended in the introduction. Heat the oil in a frying pan and fry the onion until just soft. Add the garlic and fry for 1 minute. Add the mince and fry until brown.
▎Stir in the pepper, mushrooms, tomatoes and tomato purée and bring to the boil, then simmer for 30 minutes.
▎When the potatoes are cooked, cut a wedge out of each one. Scoop out the flesh and mash with the butter and cream until smooth. Fill each potato skin half full with the mash and spoon in hot mince until it just overflows. Sprinkle with parsley and serve.

TIME: *Preparation takes about 10 minutes.*
Cooking takes approximately 40 minutes.

Easy Chilli

SERVES 4

This filling is simple to prepare

INGREDIENTS

4 large baking potatoes

15ml/1 tbsp sunflower oil

1 small onion, chopped

350g/12oz lean minced beef

5ml/1 tsp chilli powder

150ml/5 fl oz beef stock

200g/7oz can red kidney beans, drained and rinsed

400g/14oz can chopped tomatoes

15ml/1 tbsp tomato purée

▎Begin by setting the potatoes to bake in a hot oven as recommended in the introduction.
▎Heat the oil in a saucepan and fry the onion until soft. Add the meat and cook until browned.
▎Stir in the chilli powder and cook for 1 minute.
▎Stir the stock, beans, tomatoes and tomato purée into the pan and bring gently to the boil.
▎Reduce the heat and simmer for 20 minutes or until the meat is tender.
▎When the potatoes are cooked, cut the tops off, mash the flesh and pour the chilli over the top.

TIME: *Preparation takes about 5 minutes.*
Cooking takes approximately 35 minutes.

Meat and Poultry

Sausage, Egg & Bacon Jackets

SERVES 4

This traditional and popular combination is an unusual way of serving potatoes

INGREDIENTS

4 large baking potatoes
6 pork chipolatas
6 rashers streaky bacon
25g/1oz butter
20ml/4 tsp brown fruity sauce
2 hard-boiled eggs, roughly chopped

▍Begin by setting the potatoes to bake in a hot oven as recommended in the introduction.

▍Cut the chipolatas in half to form smaller sausages.

▍Remove the rind from the bacon and discard. Stretch the bacon with the back of a knife and cut each rasher into two pieces.

▍Wrap each sausage in a piece of bacon and thread 3 sausages on one cocktail stick, to make 4 mini kebabs.

▍Place on a baking sheet and cook alongside the potatoes for 25 minutes, or cook under a preheated grill.

▍Cut the tops off the cooked potatoes and scoop the flesh into a bowl. Mash well with the butter and fruity sauce.

▍Stir in the chopped egg. Spoon back into the potato skins and return to the oven for 10 minutes.

▍Top the potatoes with the sausage kebabs and serve with baked beans.

TIME: *Preparation takes about 10 minutes. Cooking takes approximately 10 minutes, plus reheating.*

MICROWAVE NOTES: *If cooking the potatoes in a microwave, reheat for 2–3 minutes on 100% (high).*

Meat and Poultry

Grilled Chicken with Garlic Butter

SERVES 4

For a more subtle flavour you can use less garlic if you wish

INGREDIENTS

4 large baking potatoes
175g/6oz unsalted butter
4 cloves garlic
salt and pepper
4 skinned chicken breasts
125ml/4fl oz thick Greek yoghurt

▌Begin by setting the potatoes to bake in a hot oven as recommended in the introduction.
▌Remove the butter from the fridge and allow it to come to room temperature.
▌Peel the garlic, place on a non-absorbent surface and roughly chop. Sprinkle with a little salt and, using the side of the knife, crush the garlic under the blade and slowly work it into a paste.
▌Place the garlic paste in a mixing bowl with the butter and beat well until they are thoroughly combined.

▌Lay the chicken breasts on a foil-covered baking sheet and season well with salt and freshly ground black pepper. Smear two-thirds of the garlic butter all over the meat.
▌When the potatoes are three-quarters cooked, place the prepared chicken under a preheated grill and cook for 10 minutes on each side or until browned.
▌Make a deep cut into each baked potato and rub some of the remaining garlic butter over the surface of the flesh, then place a piece of grilled chicken into each potato and top with a spoonful of Greek yoghurt.
▌Finish with a twist of fresh black pepper and serve immediately.

TIME: *Preparation takes about 15 minutes. Cooking takes approximately 20 minutes.*

Meat and Poultry

Chinese Beef & Green Pepper

SERVES 4

A *popular Chinese dish that lends itself very well to baked potatoes*

INGREDIENTS

4 large baking potatoes
450g/1lb fillet steak
25ml/1floz sherry
25ml/1floz soy sauce
15ml/1tbsp cornflour
45ml/3tbsp oil
2 seeded and chopped green peppers
25ml/1floz oyster sauce
meat stock

▌ Begin by setting the potatoes to bake in a hot oven as recommended in the introduction.

▌ Cut the beef into 5cm/2in slices across the grain and place in a mixing bowl. Combine the sherry, soy sauce and cornflour and pour over the sliced beef, mix well to ensure it is fully combined and set aside to marinate.

▌ When the potatoes are cooked, remove the beef from the marinade and drain off any excess liquid. Heat 30ml/2tbsp oil in a wok and quickly stir-fry the beef for about 1 minute or until just cooked, remove from the wok and set aside.

▌ Heat the remaining oil and add the chopped pepper to the pan. Stir fry until the pepper begins to soften; then return the beef to the pan along with the oyster sauce and sufficient stock to make a small amount of gravy.

▌ Toss together briefly until thoroughly heated through, then remove the wok from the heat. Make a deep cut into the potatoes and fluff up the flesh with a fork, spoon the filling into the potatoes and serve immediately.

TIME: *Preparation takes about 15 minutes.*
Marinate for at least 1 hour.
Cooking takes approximately 5 minutes.

Meat and Poultry

Italian Ham & Cheese

SERVES 4

A *quick and easy filling with a decidedly Continental feel*

INGREDIENTS

4 large baking potatoes
125g/4oz fresh Parmesan cheese
50g/2oz butter
4 slices Parma ham, cut into thin strips
10ml/2 tsp horseradish sauce
125ml/4fl oz fresh soured cream

▌Begin by setting the potatoes to bake in a hot oven as recommended in the introduction.

▌Using a potato peeler, thinly slice the Parmesan cheese into wafer-thin slivers.

▌When the potatoes are cooked, cut in half and scoop out the flesh. Mash well with the butter.

▌Reserve a little of the cheese, and beat the remainder into the potato along with the ham and horseradish sauce.

▌Pile the potato mixture back into the potato skins and return to the oven for 10 minutes to heat through.

▌Place on a serving dish and top with the soured cream and reserved cheese. Serve immediately.

TIME: *Preparation takes about 5 minutes. Reheating takes approximately 10 minutes.*
MICROWAVE NOTES: *If cooking the potatoes in a microwave, reheat for 1 minute.*

Meat and Poultry

Crunchy Chicken
SERVES 4

This dish is great for using up leftover chicken

INGREDIENTS

4 large baking potatoes

450g/1lb cooked chicken, cut into bite-sized pieces

4 small sticks celery, thinly sliced or chopped

125g/4oz sweetcorn kernels, defrosted if frozen

125ml/4fl oz Greek yoghurt

salt and pepper

30ml/2 tbsp chopped fresh mint

few drops of Tabasco sauce

fresh mint leaves for garnish

▌ Begin by setting the potatoes to bake in a hot oven as recommended in the introduction.

▌ Put the chicken, celery and sweetcorn in a bowl.

▌ Mix together the yoghurt, seasoning, chopped mint and Tabasco, and pour over the chicken mixture, stirring until well coated.

▌ When the potatoes are cooked, cut in half and mash the flesh slightly. Spoon the chicken mixture on top, garnish with fresh mint and serve immediately.

TIME: *Preparation takes about 5 minutes.*
VARIATION: *Use ham if you do not have any leftover chicken. Cooked turkey can also be used, making this an ideal Boxing Day lunch.*

Cheese & Bacon
SERVES 4

An ideal midweek supper dish

INGREDIENTS

4 large baking potatoes

225g/8oz bacon, diced

2 small onions, finely chopped

75ml/3fl oz sunflower oil

salt and pepper

125g/4oz Gruyère cheese, grated

60ml/4 tbsp fresh breadcrumbs

▌ Begin by setting the potatoes to bake in a hot oven as recommended in the introduction.

▌ Mix together the bacon and onion.

▌ Heat the oil in a frying pan and fry the bacon and onion gently for 5 minutes.

▌ Drain off any liquid, then increase the heat and cook for about 5 minutes or until beginning to crisp.

▌ Cut the cooked potato in half and scoop out the flesh into a bowl. Mash well.

▌ Beat the bacon and onion into the potato and season to taste with salt and pepper. Mix in half the cheese, then pile back into the potato skins.

▌ Mix the remaining cheese with the breadcrumbs and sprinkle over the potatoes. Place under a preheated grill until golden.

TIME: *Preparation takes about 10 minutes. Cooking takes approximately 15 minutes.*

Mini Saté & Peanut Sauce

SERVES 4

The potatoes are topped with beef kebabs and an aromatic sauce

INGREDIENTS

4 large baking potatoes
225g/8oz fillet or sirloin steak, cut into small cubes
Grated zest and juice of ½ lime
45ml/3 tbsp sunflower oil
2.5ml/½ tsp crushed dried chillies
pinch of turmeric
pinch of cumin
1 small onion, chopped
1.75ml/¼ tsp chilli powder
90ml/6 tbsp peanut butter
salt and pepper
fresh coriander, to garnish

▌Begin by setting the potatoes to bake in a hot oven as recommended in the introduction.

▌Thread the steak onto 8 cocktail sticks. Place in a shallow dish. Mix together the lime zest, juice, 30ml/2 tbsp of the oil, chillies, turmeric and cumin. Pour over the meat.

▌Allow the meat to marinate for 30 minutes, turning occasionally.

▌Heat the remaining oil in a small saucepan and fry the onion until soft.

▌Add the chilli powder and fry for 1 minute, then stir in 90ml/6 tbsp water and the peanut butter. Simmer gently for 5 minutes, stirring occasionally.

▌Cook the kebabs under a preheated grill for 5–10 minutes, turning once.

▌When the potatoes are cooked, cut the tops off each one and scoop the flesh into a bowl. Mash well. Season with salt and pepper and pile back into the potato skins. Spoon the peanut sauce on top and sprinkle with a little chopped fresh coriander. Serve with the kebabs and garnish with a sprig of coriander.

TIME: *Preparation takes about 10 minutes plus 30 minutes marinating. Cooking takes approximately 15 minutes.*

VARIATION: *Use skinned and boned chicken breasts in place of the steak.*

Meat and Poultry

Fragrant Lamb in Rosemary Gravy

SERVES 4

Using fresh herbs in the marinade intensifies the wonderful flavours

INGREDIENTS

4 large baking potatoes
2 cloves garlic
salt and pepper
25ml/1fl oz olive oil
50ml/2fl oz dry white wine
juice and zest of ½ lemon
2tbsp chopped fresh rosemary
350g/12oz fresh lamb fillet
5ml/1 tsp cornflour
butter

▌Begin by setting the potatoes to bake in a hot oven as recommended in the introduction.

▌Peel and roughly chop the garlic, sprinkle with a little salt and crush to a smooth paste with the handle of a knife. Mix the garlic paste with the olive oil, white wine and the juice and zest of the lemon.

▌Bruise the rosemary with the handle of a knife and add to the marinade.

▌Slice the lamb into 6mm/¼in slices and pour over the marinade, leave for an hour for the flavours to infuse.

▌When the potatoes are nearly cooked, remove the lamb from the marinade and arrange it on a baking sheet, season generously with salt and fresh black pepper.

▌Place under a preheated grill and cook until there is just a slight pinkness left in the centre of the lamb, turning once during cooking.

▌Whilst the lamb is grilling, heat the marinade in a saucepan and thicken with a little cornflour made into a paste with cold water, season with salt and pepper and keep hot.

▌Cut a deep cross into the baked potatoes and squeeze gently from the base of the potato to expose the flesh, than melt a little butter in each one. Share the cooked lamb between the potatoes and pour over the thickened gravy, garnish with a sprig of fresh rosemary and serve immediately.

TIME: *Preparation takes about 10 minutes.*
Marinate for at least 1 hour.
Cooking takes approximately 15 minutes.

Meat and Poultry

Barbecued Belly of Pork

SERVES 4

T*he barbecue sauce really brings out the flavours of the meat*

INGREDIENTS

4 large baking potatoes
450g/1lb lean belly of pork
butter

FOR THE BARBECUE SAUCE:

15ml/1tbsp clear honey
30ml/2tbsp thin-cut marmalade
30ml/2tbsp soy sauce
15ml/1tbsp white wine vinegar
5ml/1tsp paprika
1 clove garlic, crushed
tomato ketchup to taste

▌Cut away any little pieces of bone remaining on the belly of pork and remove the skin – this is best achieved using a pair of kitchen scissors.

▌Cut each length of pork crosswise into roughly 3cm/1½ inch lengths and place in a bowl.

▌Mix all the barbecue sauce ingredients together and pour over the prepared pork, stir together well and allow to stand for a good while so the flavours can infuse.

▌Set the potatoes to bake as recommended in the introduction.

▌When the potatoes are three-quarters cooked, remove the pork from the barbecue sauce and arrange on a foil-covered baking sheet.

▌Place under a preheated grill and cook for approximately 15 minutes, turning regularly and brushing with any remaining barbecue sauce, until the meat is nicely browned and crispy.

▌Cut a deep cross into each baked potato and melt a little butter into the flesh, share the barbecued pork evenly between the potatoes and serve immediately.

TIME: *Preparation takes about 15 minutes.*
Marinate for at least 30 minutes.
Cooking takes approximately 15 minutes.

Meat and Poultry

Chicken & Apricot Curry

Serves 4

Spicy curries go as well with potatoes as they do with their traditional accompaniment – rice

Ingredients

4 large baking potatoes
2.5ml/½ tsp chilli powder
10ml/2 tsp garam masala
2.5 cm/1 inch piece root ginger, peeled and grated
salt
2 cloves garlic, crushed
4 chicken breasts, skinned, boned and cut into bite-size pieces
30ml/2 tbsp ghee or sunflower oil
15ml/1 tbsp curry paste
1 large onion, cut into wedges
400g/14oz can chopped tomatoes
50g/2oz no-soak dried apricots, chopped
5ml/1 tsp sugar
20ml/4 tsp white wine vinegar

▮ Begin by setting the potatoes to bake in a hot oven as recommended in the introduction.

▮ Mix together the chilli powder, garam masala, ginger, salt and garlic. Spread this over the chicken, and toss to coat well.

▮ Allow the chicken to marinate for 1–2 hours to absorb the flavours.

▮ Melt the ghee or heat the oil in a large frying pan and add the spiced chicken and the curry paste.

▮ Toss over a high heat for 5 minutes until the chicken is browned.

▮ Remove from the pan and set aside.

▮ Add the onion along with a little more ghee or oil if necessary, and fry for 5 minutes until just softened.

▮ Return the chicken to the pan and add the tomatoes and apricots. Cook for 20 minutes.

▮ Stir in the sugar and vinegar, and cook for a further 10 minutes.

▮ Split the potatoes in half and top with the curry.

TIME: *Preparation takes about 15 minutes plus 2 hours marinating.*
Cooking takes approximately 40 minutes.
VARIATION: *Diced turkey can be used in this recipe in place of the chicken.*
SERVING IDEA: *This dish is delicious served with a tomato and onion salad.*

Meat and Poultry

Broad Beans & Bacon

SERVES 4

Broad beans and bacon make a delicious combination

INGREDIENTS

4 large baking potatoes
30ml/2 tbsp sunflower oil
1 onion, chopped
1 clove garlic, crushed
125g/4oz diced bacon (smoked if possible)
175g/6oz frozen broad beans
salt and pepper
15ml/1 tbsp chopped fresh mixed herbs
or 5ml/1 tsp dried mixed herbs
60g/2oz Cheddar cheese, grated
30ml/2 tbsp grated Parmesan cheese
fresh herbs to garnish

▌ Begin by setting the potatoes to bake in a hot oven as recommended in the introduction.

▌ Heat the oil in a frying pan and fry the onion for 3–4 minutes or until beginning to soften.

▌ Add the garlic and fry gently for 1 minute.

▌ Increase the heat and add the bacon, then fry for about 5 minutes or until beginning to crisp.

▌ Cook the beans in boiling water for 3–4 minutes, drain well and add to the pan. Stir in the salt, pepper and herbs.

▌ When the potatoes are cooked, cut in half and scoop out the flesh. Mash well.

▌ Mix the beans and bacon into the potato and pile back into the potato skins.

▌ Mix together the two cheeses and sprinkle over the potatoes. Brown under a preheated grill and serve immediately. Garnish with mixed herbs.

TIME: *Preparation takes about 10 minutes. Cooking takes approximately 15 minutes.*
SERVING IDEA: *Serve as a light meal or as an accompaniment to other dishes.*

Meat and Poultry

Calves Liver with Sweet Red Onions

SERVES 4

A *delightful mix of savoury and sweet flavours*

INGREDIENTS

4 large baking potatoes
700g/1½lb calves liver
2 egg yolks, lightly beaten
brown breadcrumbs for coating
salt and black pepper
olive oil
450g/1lb red onions, peeled and finely sliced
15ml/1tbsp demerara sugar

▌Set the potatoes to bake in a hot oven as recommended in the introduction.

▌When the potatoes are three-quarters cooked, begin preparing the topping.

▌Rinse the liver under cold running water and pat dry with absorbent kitchen paper, then slice into strips of roughly equal sizes.

▌Place the egg yolks and breadcrumbs with a little seasoning in separate bowls. Dip each piece of liver in the egg yolk and then coat thoroughly with the seasoned crumbs. Arrange the prepared liver on a lightly oiled baking sheet and set aside.

▌Heat 30ml/½tbsp of olive oil and gently fry the onions until soft and slightly browned, stir in the demerara sugar and remove from the heat.

▌Place the crumbed liver under a preheated grill for approximately 6 minutes, carefully turning once during cooking. The cooked liver should remain pink on the inside but crisp and golden on the outside.

▌Cut a deep cross in the top of each baked potato and gently squeeze from the base so the fluffy potato flesh is exposed.

▌Spoon the onion and cooking juices followed by the crisp liver over the top of each potato, finish with a twist of freshly ground pepper and serve.

TIME: *Preparation takes about 15 minutes. Cooking takes approximately 10 minutes.*

Smoked Haddock & Tomato

SERVES 4

Smoked fish gives a lovely flavour to potatoes

INGREDIENTS

4 large baking potatoes
225g/8oz smoked haddock, skinned
60ml/4 tbsp milk
knob of butter
salt and pepper
pinch of grated nutmeg
1 beef tomato, chopped
5ml/1 tsp chopped fresh parsley
fresh parsley to garnish

▎Begin by setting the potatoes to bake in a hot oven as recommended in the introduction.

▎Put the haddock in an ovenproof dish. Pour over the milk and add the butter. Season with salt and pepper. Cover with foil.

▎About 20 minutes before the end of the potatoes' cooking time, place the fish on a lower shelf in the oven. Cook until it flakes easily with a fork.

▎Cut a lid off the cooked potatoes and discard. Scoop out the flesh and place in a large bowl. Carefully add the liquid from the fish and the nutmeg. Season to taste and mash well.

▎Beat the tomato pieces into the potato along with the chopped parsley.

▎Pile the potato flesh back into the skins.

▎Pile the flaked fish on top of the potato and serve garnished with fresh parsley.

TIME: *Preparation takes about 10 minutes. Cooking takes approximately 20 minutes.*
VARIATION: *Use another smoked fish in this recipe, such as kipper, smoked mackerel or smoked cod.*
COOK'S TIP: *Cooking the fish in the oven at the same time as the potatoes is a good way of saving fuel.*
MICROWAVE NOTES: *This recipe is not suitable for cooking in a microwave.*

Fish

Prawn & Avocado

SERVES 4

You can use smaller potatoes and serve this dish as a starter

INGREDIENTS

4 large baking potatoes
1 ripe avocado, peeled and cubed
grated zest and juice of ½ lime
125g/4oz cooked and peeled prawns
1 tomato, skinned and chopped
60ml/4 tbsp Greek yoghurt
15ml/1 tbsp tomato purée
dash of Tabasco
salt and pepper
ground paprika

▍Begin by setting the potatoes to bake in a hot oven as recommended in the introduction.
▍Toss the avocado pieces in the lime juice to prevent discoloration.
▍Add the prawns and tomato and stir to combine.
▍In a small mixing bowl, mix together the yoghurt, tomato purée, Tabasco, seasoning and lime zest.
▍Pour over the prawns and toss until well coated.
▍When the potatoes are cooked, cut a cross in the top of each one. Gently squeeze each potato to open out the cross slightly.
▍Pile the prawns on top and garnish with a sprinkling of paprika.

TIME: *Preparation takes about 15 minutes.*
WATCHPOINT: *Avocados are ripe when they yield slightly upon being gently squeezed. If very soft, they will be mushy and will not have a good flavour.*

Fish

Scrambled Eggs & Smoked Salmon

SERVES 4

An ideal special supper or brunch dish

INGREDIENTS

4 large baking potatoes

4 eggs

60ml/4 tbsp milk

salt and pepper

pinch of grated nutmeg

pinch of cayenne pepper

175g/6oz butter

225g/8oz smoked salmon, cut into strips

1 bunch chives, snipped

grilled tomatoes and fresh chives to serve

▎Begin by setting the potatoes to bake in a hot oven.
▎Put the eggs in a small bowl with the milk, seasoning, nutmeg and cayenne and beat with a fork until frothy.
▎When the potatoes are cooked, cut in half and dot with a little butter. Mash the flesh and keep warm.
▎Melt the remaining butter in a small saucepan and pour in the egg mixture. Cook over a low heat, stirring constantly, to scramble the egg as it cooks.
▎When almost set, stir in the smoked salmon and chives and cook for a few seconds. Pile onto the potatoes and serve with grilled tomatoes and garnish with fresh chives.

TIME: *Preparation takes about 5 minutes.*
Cooking takes approximately 5 minutes.

Piquant Flaked Salmon

SERVES 4

The perfect healthy lunchtime snack

INGREDIENTS

4 large baking potatoes

400g/14oz can red salmon, drained

75ml/3fl oz white wine vinegar

juice of ½ lime

black pepper

roughly chopped coriander to garnish

▎Begin by setting the potatoes to bake in a hot oven as recommended in the introduction.
▎Carefully remove the salmon from the can and place it in a bowl. Using a fork break it into its natural flakes.
▎Put the wine vinegar, lime juice and black pepper into a screw top jar and shake well to mix it together. Pour the mixture over the salmon and allow it to soak into the fish while the potatoes finish baking.
▎When the potatoes are cooked, split them down the centre and share the salmon between them, garnish each potato with plenty of chopped coriander and serve.

TIME: *Preparation takes about 5 minutes.*

Fish

Fresh Steamed Mussels with Parsley

SERVES 4

A *great lunchtime dish, so evocative of rustic French cafés*

INGREDIENTS

1¼ litre/2pts small fresh mussels

4 large baking potatoes

50g/2oz butter

1 large onion, finely chopped

150ml/5floz white wine

75ml/3floz soured cream

fresh parsley, chopped

▌ If time allows it is a good idea to feed the mussels for 24 hours prior to cooking as this removes any impurities that may be inside the shell. To do this, scrub the shells thoroughly, place the mussels in a bowl of fresh cold water and sprinkle a small amount of flour over the surface of the water.

▌ Set the potatoes to bake in a hot oven as recommended in the introduction.

▌ When the potatoes are nearly cooked, melt the butter in a large saucepan with a tight-fitting lid and fry the onion until soft but not coloured.

▌ Drain the water from the mussels and rinse well. Discard any that have already opened.

▌ Add the mussels to the saucepan along with the white wine and cover with the lid, increase the heat and allow a few minutes for the mussels to steam.

▌ When the majority of shells have opened and the mussels inside are a wonderful pink/orange colour remove the pan from the heat.

▌ Split the baked potatoes down the centre and, using a slotted spoon, divide the cooked mussels between the four potatoes. Any shells that remain closed should be discarded.

▌ Quickly reheat the cooking liquor and stir in the soured cream, gently warm it through before pouring a little over each potato.

▌ Finish with a generous handful of chopped parsley and serve with crusty French bread.

TIME: *Allow 24 hours for the mussels to clean. Cooking takes approximately 5–10 minutes.*

Fish

Kipper & Egg Mash
SERVES 4

This first-rate fish dish is ideal for brunch

INGREDIENTS
4 large baking potatoes
2 pairs fresh kippers
butter
2 hard-boiled eggs, roughly chopped
175g/3oz frozen peas, defrosted
salt and pepper
60ml/4 tbsp grated red Leicester cheese
60ml/4 tbsp grated Cheddar cheese
Hard-boiled egg slices and sprigs of dill, to garnish

▌Begin by setting the potatoes to bake in a hot oven as recommended in the introduction.
▌Dot the fish with butter and wrap them in foil, place in a preheated oven 180°C/350°F/Gas Mark 4 for 20 minutes.
▌Put the chopped egg in a mixing bowl with the peas. When the fish is cooked pour the juices over the egg and peas.
▌Carefully remove all the flesh from the kippers, flake it into pieces and add it to the bowl.
▌When the potatoes are cooked, cut in half and scoop out the flesh. Mash well and add to the fish.
▌Beat the fish and potato together until well combined. Taste and season as desired.
▌Pile back into the potato skins. Mix together the two cheeses and sprinkle on top. Return to the oven for 10–15 minutes to heat through and brown the cheese.
▌Serve garnished with egg slices and sprigs of dill.

TIME: *Preparation takes about 5 minutes. Cooking takes approximately 30 minutes.*
MICROWAVE NOTES: *If cooking the potatoes in a microwave, reheat for $1\frac{1}{2}$ minutes on 100% (high).*

Fish

King Prawns in Lime & Dill Mayonnaise

SERVES 4

This fresh-tasting mayonnaise tastes great with fish

INGREDIENTS

4 large baking potatoes
60ml/4 tbsp chopped fresh dill
90ml/3 fl oz olive oil
juice of ½ lemon
salt and pepper
20 large cooked prawns, shelled
juice and zest of 1 lime
300ml/10 fl oz fresh mayonnaise
12 cherry tomatoes, halved
dill sprigs and lime segments to garnish

▌Begin by setting the potatoes to bake in a hot oven as recommended in the introduction.

▌Mix together 30ml/2 tbsp of the chopped dill, olive oil, lemon juice and seasoning and pour over the prawns. Put to one side whilst the flavours infuse.

▌Add the juice and zest of the lime and the remaining chopped dill to the mayonnaise, season with some black pepper and beat together thoroughly. Chill in the refrigerator until required.

▌When the potatoes are cooked drain the marinade from the prawns and combine them with the tomato halves and the mayonnaise.

▌Cut the potatoes almost in half and lightly break up the flesh with a fork. Spoon the filling carefully over each potato.

▌Garnish with sprigs of dill and serve with segments of lime and a twist of fresh pepper.

TIME: *Preparation takes about 10 minutes. Marinate for at least 45 minutes.*

Fish

Tuna with Multi-coloured Peppers

SERVES 4

The *ginger in this recipe gives it a slightly exotic flavour*

INGREDIENTS

4 large baking potatoes
30ml/2 tbsp olive oil
½ green pepper, seeded and diced
½ red pepper, seeded and diced
½ yellow pepper, seeded and diced
2.5ml/½ tsp black or white pepper
2.5cm/1 inch piece root ginger, peeled and grated
2.5ml/½ tsp crushed dried chillies
salt and pepper
200g/7oz can tuna chunks, drained
grated zest of ½ lemon
15ml/1 tbsp lemon juice
60g/2oz Cheddar cheese, grated

▌Begin by setting the potatoes to bake in a hot oven as recommended in the introduction.

▌Heat the oil in a frying pan and toss the peppers in the oil. Cook over a moderate heat for 5 minutes, stirring regularly until soft and beginning to brown slightly.

▌Add the ginger and crushed chillies, and season with salt and pepper.

▌Add the tuna, lemon zest and juice to the pan. Cook over a low heat for 2–3 minutes or until the tuna is hot.

▌When the potatoes are cooked, cut in half and scoop the flesh into a bowl. Mash well.

▌Add the tuna mixture to the potato and mix well.

▌Pile back into the potato skins and sprinkle with grated cheese. Return to the oven for 10 minutes or until the cheese melts.

TIME: *Preparation takes about 10 minutes. Cooking takes approximately 15 minutes plus reheating.*

VARIATION: *Use canned salmon in place of the tuna.*

MICROWAVE NOTES: *If cooking the potatoes in a microwave, reheat for 2–3 minutes on 100% (high).*

Fish

Rolled Fresh Anchovies

SERVES 4

Full of the tastes of the Mediterranean

INGREDIENTS

4 large baking potatoes

16 fresh anchovies, filleted

6 fresh red chillies, seeded and finely sliced

300ml/10fl oz virgin olive oil

16 pitted black olives

unsalted butter

▌Begin by setting the potatoes to bake in a hot oven as recommended in the introduction.

▌Add chilli slices to the olive oil. For a really good chilli oil it is best to leave the chillies marinating for at least 10 days; however this is not essential and the oil can be used quite soon after being prepared.

▌Roll each anchovy around an olive and spike them through with a cocktail stick. Place on a dish and pour over the chilli oil. Leave to marinate.

▌When the potatoes are cooked, cut a deep cross into each one and gently push from the base of the potato to expose the flesh. Place a knob of butter on each potato and lay 4 of the marinated anchovies on top, pour over 5ml/1 tsp of the flavoured marinade and serve at once.

TIME: *Preparation takes about 10 minutes. Marinate for at least 30 minutes.*

COOK'S TIP: *Do not be put off using anchovies in this way as their flavour is much more subtle than that of the tinned variety.*

Sardine & Tomato Hash

SERVES 4

A simple stand-by meal

INGREDIENTS

4 large baking potatoes

30ml/2 tbsp olive oil

1 bunch spring onions, sliced

4 cloves garlic, crushed

4 sticks celery, chopped

few fresh basil leaves

2 x 400g/14oz cans sardines in tomato sauce

salt and pepper

knob of butter

dash of Worcestershire sauce

▌Begin by setting the potatoes to bake in a hot oven as recommended in the introduction.

▌Heat the oil in a small pan and fry the spring onions and garlic for 2–3 minutes or until the onions are soft.

▌Add the celery and cook for another 3–4 minutes.

▌Tear the basil into small pieces and add to the pan along with the sardines in their sauce. Mix well. Season and add the butter and Worcestershire sauce.

▌When the potatoes are cooked, scoop out the flesh, keeping it as whole as possible, and cut into cubes.

▌Add to the pan and toss over the heat for a few minutes before piling back into the potato skins. Serve immediately.

TIME: *Preparation takes about 10 minutes. Cooking takes approximately 20 minutes.*

Fish

Seafood & Tomato

SERVES 4

Prepared, mixed seafood is readily available

INGREDIENTS

4 large baking potatoes
30ml/2 tbsp sunflower oil
1 clove garlic, crushed
350g/12oz tomatoes, skinned and chopped
75ml/5 tbsp white wine
450g/1lb mixed seafood, e.g. squid, mussels, prawns
30ml/2 tbsp chopped fresh parsley

- Begin by setting the potatoes to bake in a hot oven as recommended in the introduction.
- Heat the oil in a saucepan and fry the garlic.
- Add the tomatoes and sauté for 2 minutes, then stir in the wine and bring to the boil.
- Reduce the heat and simmer for 30 minutes or until thickened slightly.
- Stir in the seafood and simmer gently for 10 minutes or until piping hot. Stir in the parsley.
- If the sauce is still runny, thicken with a little cornflour, mixed to a paste with cold water.
- When the potatoes are cooked, cut in half and mash the flesh slightly if liked. Spoon the seafood mixture on top and serve immediately.

TIME: *Preparation takes about 10 minutes. Cooking takes approximately 45 minutes.*

Tangy Crab & Prawn

SERVES 4

A light and attractive seafood dish

INGREDIENTS

4 large baking potatoes
300g/10oz can crab-meat, drained
125g/4oz cooked and peeled prawns
1 bunch spring onions, sliced
250ml/8fl oz mayonnaise
grated zest and juice of 1 lime
salt and pepper

- Begin by setting the potatoes to bake in a hot oven as recommended in the introduction.
- Put the crab-meat in a bowl and stir in the prawns and sliced spring onions.
- Mix together the mayonnaise, lime zest and juice. Pour over the fish and stir until well combined. Season to taste with salt and pepper.
- When the potatoes are cooked, cut in half, scoop out the flesh and mash well.
- Pile back into the potato skins and top with the crab mixture.

TIME: *Preparation takes about 5 minutes.*
VARIATION: *Use crab sticks if preferred.*

Fish

Calamari in Spinach & Cream Sauce

SERVES 4

A *great-tasting fish in a delicious, colourful sauce*

INGREDIENTS

4 large baking potatoes
16oz/1lb small fresh squid, cleaned (with quills removed)
50ml/2fl oz olive oil
1 onion, finely chopped
2 cloves garlic
75g/3oz frozen spinach, defrosted
300ml/10fl oz double cream
salt and pepper
fresh chopped parsley

▎Begin by setting the potatoes to bake in a hot oven as recommended in the introduction.

▎Wash the squid under cold running water and pat dry with absorbent kitchen paper, cut into 5mm/¼ inch rings and set to one side.

▎When the potatoes are nearly cooked heat 30ml/2 tbsp olive oil in a frying pan and fry the chopped onion until soft but not coloured. Skin and crush the garlic and add to the pan, frying for a further minute.

▎Squeeze as much liquid from the spinach as possible before adding it to the pan and heating through. Stir in the cream, season well with salt and fresh black pepper and throw in a handful of chopped parsley. Allow to simmer for a further minute or two, stirring to combine all the flavours, then reduce the heat to a very low simmer.

▎Heat the remainder of the olive oil in a separate pan and add the squid rings, cook until the liquid has run from the fish. This will only take a couple of minutes.

▎Drain the liquid from the squid and stir the fish into the cream sauce, increase the heat and allow the sauce to simmer gently for a further five minutes.

▎Split the baked potatoes through the middle and share the sauce between them, finish with a little more chopped parsley and serve immediately.

TIME: *Preparation takes about 5 minutes.*
Cooking takes approximately 15 minutes.

Fish

Deep-fried Devilled Whitebait

SERVES 4

Cripsy whitebait makes an unusual potato filling

INGREDIENTS

4 large baking potatoes

450g/1lb whitebait

125ml/4floz milk

oil for frying

2 lemons

FOR THE COATING:

12g/½oz flour

5ml/1 tsp English mustard powder

5ml/1 tsp cayenne pepper

pinch of ground ginger

salt and pepper

▍Begin by setting the potatoes to bake in a hot oven as recommended in the introduction.

▍When the potatoes are nearly cooked, rinse the whitebait under cold water and drop them into the milk.

▍Mix together the ingredients for the coating and pass it through a sieve to remove any lumps. Drain any excess milk from the fish and mix them into the coating.

▍Heat the oil for deep frying. A simple test to check that the oil is hot enough is to drop a small cube of bread into the pan – if it browns within 30 seconds the oil has reached the correct temperature.

▍Shake the whitebait in a sieve to remove any excess coating and fry the fish in several batches to prevent them sticking together. Keep the cooked fish warm in the oven whilst frying the remainder.

▍Cut a deep cross into each potato and gently ease it open, loosen the flesh with a fork and melt a generous portion of butter over it.

▍Share the whitebait between the potatoes and finish the dish with a little fresh black pepper and wedge of lemon before serving.

TIME: *Preparation takes about 10 minutes. Cooking takes approximately 10 minutes.*

Vegetables

Mixed Bean Salad Jackets

SERVES 4

The beans turn simple jacket potatoes into a wholesome and filling meal

INGREDIENTS

4 large baking potatoes

225g/8oz can red kidney beans, drained and rinsed

225g/8oz can butter beans, drained and rinsed

½ x 432g/16oz can aduki beans, drained and rinsed

½ x 400g/14oz can cut green beans, drained and rinsed

60g/2oz sweetcorn kernels, defrosted

2 sticks celery, sliced

1 clove garlic

2.5ml/½ tsp salt

5ml/1 tsp mustard powder

15ml/1 tbsp cider vinegar

freshly ground black pepper

90ml/6 tbsp olive oil

5ml/1 tsp snipped fresh chives

5ml/1 tsp chopped fresh tarragon

5ml/1 tsp chopped fresh parsley

knob of butter

▌Begin by setting the potatoes to bake in a hot oven as recommended in the introduction.

▌Put the beans in a bowl and toss to mix. Stir in the sweetcorn and celery.

▌Using a pestle and mortar, pound the garlic and salt to a paste. Add the mustard powder, vinegar and pepper and mix thoroughly. Gradually blend in the olive oil.

▌Transfer the garlic mixture to a small cup and add the herbs, whisking with a fork until well blended.

▌Pour over the beans and toss until all the beans are well coated in the dressing.

▌When the potatoes are cooked, cut the tops off each one and scoop out the flesh.

▌Add a knob of butter and sprinkle with a little black pepper. Mash well. Pile back into the potato skins and serve with the bean salad.

TIME: *Preparation takes about 10 minutes.*

Vegetables

Welsh Tatties

SERVES 4

These potatoes are filled with leeks and a creamy cheese sauce

INGREDIENTS

4 large baking potatoes

50g/2oz butter

450g/1lb leeks, thinly sliced

25g/1oz plain flour

300ml/10fl oz pint milk

90g/3oz Caerphilly cheese, crumbled

salt and pepper

cherry tomatoes to garnish

▍ Begin by setting the potatoes to bake in a hot oven as recommended in the introduction.

▍ Melt the butter in a saucepan and fry the leeks over a low heat for 6–10 minutes or until soft.

▍ Stir in the plain flour and cook for 1 minute.

▍ Remove from the heat and gradually add the milk, stirring well after each addition.

▍ Return the pan to the heat and cook over a low heat until thickened, stirring constantly.

▍ Add the cheese to the sauce, and gently cook until most of the cheese melts.

▍ When the potatoes are cooked, cut in half and scoop out the flesh. Mash well.

▍ Add the leek mixture and beat until well combined. Season to taste. Spoon back into the potato skins and serve garnished with cherry tomatoes.

TIME: *Preparation takes about 10 minutes. Cooking takes approximately 15 minutes.*

Vegetables

Spicy Vegetable Curry

SERVES 4

Curry served with jacket potatoes makes a superb winter dish which is both warming and filling

INGREDIENTS

4 large baking potatoes
30ml/2 tbsp ghee or sunflower oil
1 onion, chopped
2 cloves garlic, crushed
10ml/2 tsp ground coriander
5ml/1 tsp ground cumin
2.5ml/½ tsp ground fenugreek
2.5ml/½ tsp ground turmeric
2.5ml/½ tsp chilli powder
175g/6oz small cauliflower florets
2 carrots, sliced
1 red pepper, seeded and cut into small chunks
1 green pepper, seeded and cut into small chunks
125g/4oz mushrooms, halved or quartered
125g/4oz green beans cut into short lengths
300ml/10fl oz vegetable stock
5ml/1 tsp cornflour (optional)
60ml/4 tbsp natural yoghurt
45ml/3 tbsp crème fraîche

▌Begin by setting the potatoes to bake in a hot oven as recommended in the introduction.

▌Melt the ghee or heat the oil in a large saucepan and fry the onion for about 5 minutes or until softened.

▌Stir in the garlic and spices and cook over a low heat for 3 minutes, stirring constantly to prevent the spices from burning.

▌Add the vegetables and toss over the heat for 3–4 minutes.

▌Pour in the stock and bring to the boil. Reduce the heat, cover and simmer for 30 minutes, stirring occasionally, until the vegetables are tender.

▌Thicken the liquid with a little cornflour mixed to a paste with cold water if liked. Stir in the yoghurt and crème fraîche and heat gently.

▌When the potatoes are cooked, cut in half and mash the flesh if liked. Spoon over the curry and serve immediately.

TIME: *Preparation takes about 15 minutes. Cooking time approximately 45 minutes.*

Vegetables

Spicy Guacamole Potatoes

SERVES 4

A*dd a touch of spice to your potatoes with this Mexican dish*

INGREDIENTS

4 large baking potatoes
1 red or green chilli
½ small onion, cut into chunks
1 clove garlic, crushed
2 tomatoes, skinned, seeded and roughly chopped
2.5ml/¼ tsp ground cumin
2.5ml/¼ tsp ground coriander
1 large or 2 small ripe avocados
15ml/1 tbsp chopped coriander
15ml/1 tbsp chopped parsley
10ml/2 tsp lemon juice
pinch of sugar
salt and pepper
tomato relish and fresh soured cream, to serve

▎Begin by setting the potatoes to bake in a hot oven as recommended in the introduction.

▎Cut the chilli in half and remove the seeds if liked. The seeds have the spicy heat of the chilli and the end dish will be hotter if they are left in. Cut into chunks.

▎Put the onion, chilli and garlic in a food processor and process briefly to chop roughly.

▎Add the chopped tomato to the mixture in the food processor along with the cumin and ground coriander.

▎Cut the avocado in half lengthwise. Twist the halves gently in opposite directions to separate. Remove the stone and scoop out the flesh, scraping the skin well.

▎Add the avocado to the mixture in the food processor with the chopped coriander, parsley, lemon juice, sugar and seasoning. Process until the mixture is well combined with a fine, smooth consistency.

▎Chill until required.

▎When the potatoes are cooked, cut a cross in the top of each one. Gently squeeze each potato to open out the cross slightly.

▎Spoon the guacamole into the potatoes and top with tomato relish and soured cream.

TIME: *Preparation takes about 15 minutes.*

Vegetables

Curried Potato & Egg Jackets
Serves 4

Hard-boiled eggs are tossed in a creamy, lightly spiced sauce, then used to stuff the potato

Ingredients

4 large baking potatoes
4 hard-boiled eggs, roughly chopped
3 sticks celery, sliced
2 spring onions, sliced
1 small green pepper, seeded and chopped
5–10ml/1–2 tsp mild curry paste
30ml/2 tbsp single cream
45ml/3 tbsp mayonnaise
10ml/2 tsp mango chutney
paprika

▌Begin by setting the potatoes to bake in a hot oven as recommended in the introduction.

▌Put the chopped egg, celery, spring onions and green pepper into a mixing bowl.

▌In a small bowl mix together the curry paste, cream, mayonnaise and chutney until well combined.

▌Pour over the chopped eggs and toss until well coated.

▌When the potatoes are cooked, cut a lid off each one and scoop out the flesh. Mash well.

▌Add the potato to the egg mixture and mix well. Pile back into the potato skins and return to the oven for 10 minutes to heat through. Sprinkle with paprika and serve immediately.

TIME: *Preparation takes about 10 minutes. Reheating takes approximately 10 minutes.*
MICROWAVE NOTES: *If cooking the potatoes in a microwave, reheat for 2–3 minutes on 100% (high).*

Vegetables

Ratatouille Topping
Serves 4

Ratatouille is a Mediterranean dish which is ideal as a light meal when served on potatoes

Ingredients

4 large baking potatoes
30ml/2 tbsp olive oil
1 Spanish onion, sliced
1 clove garlic, crushed
½ small aubergine, chopped
½ red pepper, seeded and chopped
½ green pepper; seeded and chopped
400g/14oz can chopped tomatoes
15ml/1 tbsp tomato purée
5ml/1 tsp chopped fresh oregano
few fresh basil leaves, torn into pieces
75ml/5 tbsp red wine or vegetable stock
salt and pepper

- Begin by setting the potatoes to bake in a hot oven as recommended in the introduction.
- Heat the oil in a large frying pan and sauté the onion until beginning to soften. Add the garlic and cook for 1 minute.
- Stir in the aubergine and peppers and fry over a medium heat until just beginning to soften.
- Add the tomatoes, tomato purée, oregano, basil and wine or stock. Bring gently to the boil, then reduce the heat and simmer for 30 minutes or until the liquid has reduced slightly.
- When the potatoes are cooked, cut in half and place on a serving plate.
- Season the ratatouille to taste and spoon over the potatoes. Serve immediately.

TIME: *Preparation takes about 20 minutes. Cooking takes approximately 40 minutes.*

Vegetables

Red Cabbage with Cashew Nuts

SERVES 4

An unusual and appetising filling that can appeal to non-vegetarians too

INGREDIENTS

4 large baking potatoes
450g/16oz fresh red cabbage
1 onion
15ml/1tbsp brown sugar
50g/2oz cashew nuts
salt and pepper

▌Begin by setting the potatoes to bake in a hot oven as recommended in the introduction.

▌Remove the dark outer leaves from the cabbage and cut it in half through the stalk, then using a very sharp knife cut through the cabbage, across the leaves, to produce thin slices. Discard the stalk.

▌Peel and slice the onion, as thinly as possible, as it will only have the same amount of time to cook as the cabbage.

▌When the potatoes are three-quarters cooked, place the cabbage and onion slices and sufficient water to cover the base, in a saucepan with a tight-fitting lid.

▌Place over a high heat for 10–15 minutes until the cabbage has softened but still retains a certain crispness. At this point stir in the brown sugar and cashew nuts and allow to stand for a few minutes.

▌When the potatoes are cooked, remove from the oven and split them through the centre. Season the filling with plenty of salt and freshly ground black pepper and pile spoonfuls into each potato.

TIME: *Preparation takes about 10 minutes. Cooking takes approximately 20 minutes.*

Vegetables

Spinach & Cream Cheese Soufflé

SERVES 4

These cheesy potatoes have a lighter texture than traditional baked potatoes

INGREDIENTS

4 large baking potatoes
30ml/2 tbsp sunflower oil
1 small onion, finely chopped
175g/6oz fresh spinach, washed
125g/4oz cream cheese
salt and pepper
3 eggs, separated
15ml/1 tbsp pine nuts

▌Begin by setting the potatoes to bake in a hot oven as recommended in the introduction.

▌Heat the oil in a saucepan and fry the onion until softened.

▌Add the spinach with just the water that clings to the leaves after washing and cook, covered, for about 5 minutes until wilted.

▌Drain off any water and roughly chop the spinach in a food processor.

▌Beat the spinach into the cream cheese. Season to taste.

▌When the potatoes are cooked, cut the tops off each one and scoop out the flesh. Mash well.

▌Beat the spinach mixture, egg yolks and pine nuts into the mashed potatoes.

▌Whisk the egg whites until standing in soft peaks, then carefully fold into the potato.

▌Spoon the mixture back into the potato skins.

▌Return to the oven and cook for 15–20 minutes or until risen and golden. Serve immediately.

TIME: *Preparation takes about 10 minutes. Cooking takes approximately 25 minutes.*

Vegetables

Crunchy Blue Cheese & Walnut

SERVES 4

This is a lovely filling for summer jacket potatoes as it has a fresh flavour and crunchy texture

INGREDIENTS

4 large baking potatoes
1 apple, sliced
lemon juice
4 sticks celery, sliced
50g/2oz walnuts, chopped
150g/5oz tub Greek yoghurt
50g/2oz blue cheese
salt and pepper
lemon twists, to garnish

▌Begin by setting the potatoes to bake in a hot oven as recommended in the introduction.

▌Toss the sliced apple in a little lemon juice to prevent discoloration.

▌Put the celery, apple and walnuts in a bowl and add the yoghurt.

▌Crumble the blue cheese into the bowl, then toss all the ingredients together until well combined.

▌When the potatoes are cooked, cut a cross in the top of each one. Gently squeeze each potato to open out the cross slightly.

▌Season the potatoes with salt and pepper, then spoon the blue cheese mixture on top. Garnish with twists of lemon.

TIME: *Preparation takes about 10 minutes.*

Vegetables

Sultana Cauliflower Cheese

SERVES 4

A *great-tasting variation of a classic English dish*

INGREDIENTS

4 large baking potatoes
1 cauliflower
50g/2oz butter
50g/2oz flour
600ml/20fl oz milk
125g/4oz strong Cheddar cheese, grated
salt and pepper
50g/2oz sultanas

▍Begin by setting the potatoes to bake in a hot oven as recommended in the introduction.

▍Break off the outer leaves of the cauliflower and cut the heart into walnut-sized florets. Rinse them thoroughly under cold running water.

▍Bring a saucepan of salted water to the boil and cook the cauliflower florets for 5–10 minutes until just tender. Drain off the water and spread them over absorbent kitchen paper to remove any excess moisture.

▍To make the sauce, gently melt the butter in a saucepan, add the flour and allow to cook together for a minute or two. Do not allow the mixture to colour as this will affect the finished sauce.

▍Slowly add the milk a little at a time, stirring continuously until all the milk is incorporated and the sauce is smooth and thick. At this stage stir in two-thirds of the grated cheese and season generously with salt and freshly ground black pepper. Once the cheese has melted into the sauce remove the pan from the heat and set to one side.

▍Spread the blanched cauliflower over a lightly greased ovenproof dish and sprinkle with the sultanas, pour over the cheese sauce and place in a preheated oven, 180°C/350°F/Gas Mark 4, for 30 minutes.

▍Prior to serving, remove the cauliflower cheese from the oven, sprinkle with the remaining grated cheese and place under a hot grill until a bubbling brown crust forms.

▍Split the baked potatoes and spoon in lots of cauliflower and cheese sauce, add a final twist of fresh black pepper and serve.

TIME: *Preparation takes about 10 minutes. Cooking takes approximately 45 minutes.*

Vegetables

Chick Pea Curry
Serves 4

A topping with a sophisticated taste

Ingredients
4 large baking potatoes
50g/2oz butter
1 onion, finely chopped
10ml/2 tsp ground coriander
2.5ml/½ tsp turmeric
2.5ml/½ tsp chilli powder
2 x 400g/14oz cans chick peas, drained
salt
150ml/5 fl oz plain full fat yoghurt

▌Begin by setting the potatoes to bake in a hot oven as recommended in the introduction.
▌Melt the butter in a saucepan and gently fry the onion until golden brown. Add all the various spices to the pan and continue to cook briefly, then moisten with 5ml/2fl oz water and allow to heat through.
▌Add the drained chick peas and cover for a few minutes to allow the flavours to mix with the peas. Do not leave the pan for too long as the peas may begin to break up.
▌Remove the pan from the heat, season well with salt and gently stir in the yoghurt.
▌Spoon the curry into the hot potato and serve with sweet mango chutney.

TIME: *Preparation takes about 5 minutes. Cooking takes approximately 20 minutes.*

Coleslaw & Bavarian Cheese
Serves 4

Smoked cheese added to tangy coleslaw

Ingredients
4 large baking potatoes
½ small head of white cabbage, thinly shredded
2 carrots, grated
½ green pepper, seeded and thinly sliced
90g/3oz Bavarian smoked cheese
60ml/4 tbsp mayonnaise
60ml/4 tbsp fresh soured cream
salt and pepper
40ml/2 tbsp cashew nuts, toasted

▌Begin by setting the potatoes to bake in a hot oven as recommended in the introduction.
▌Put the shredded cabbage in a large mixing bowl and add the grated carrot and sliced pepper. Add the cheese.
▌Mix together the mayonnaise and cream, and season well. Pour over the cabbage and toss until all the vegetables are coated.
▌When the potatoes are cooked, cut in half and mash the flesh if liked. Serve with the coleslaw piled on top. Sprinkle with toasted cashew nuts.

TIME: *Preparation takes about 15 minutes.*

Vegetables

Grilled Goats' Cheese with Basil

SERVES 4

This recipe brings the flavours of Italy to meal times

INGREDIENTS

4 large baking potatoes
2 small goats' cheeses
virgin olive oil
salt and pepper
fresh basil leaves

▌Begin by setting the potatoes to bake in a hot oven as recommended in the introduction.

▌When the potatoes are nearly cooked, cut the cheeses into rounds and arrange them on a baking sheet. Brush each slice generously with some olive oil then turn them over, brush again and season well with plenty of salt and freshly ground black pepper.

▌Place the prepared cheese under a preheated grill and cook for a few minutes until the cheese has softened.

▌Slice the baked potatoes in half and gently fork over the inside to fluff it up a little, then carefully transfer the softened cheese slices onto the potato.

▌Finally, season once more with freshly ground black pepper and tear a few basil leaves and scatter over the potatoes before serving.

TIME: *Preparation takes about 5 minutes. Cooking takes approximately 5 minutes.*
SERVING IDEA: *This lunchtime snack has a very Mediterranean feel to it that's even more convincing served with a simple leaf salad and French dressing.*

Vegetables

Garlicky Mushroom & Hazelnuts

SERVES 4

Simple to prepare, this topping is quite irresistible

INGREDIENTS

4 large baking potatoes

90g/3oz butter

1 small onion, peeled and finely chopped

3 cloves garlic, peeled and crushed

175g/6oz small button mushrooms, quartered

45g/1½oz toasted hazelnuts, chopped

grated zest and juice of ½ lemon

salt and black pepper

30ml/2 tbsp chopped parsley

▌Set the potatoes to bake in a hot oven as recommended in the introduction.

▌Melt the butter in a frying pan and fry the onion until just softened.

▌Stir in the garlic and cook for 1 minute.

▌Add the mushrooms to the pan and fry for 4–5 minutes until softened.

▌Stir in the hazelnuts, lemon zest, juice, seasoning and parsley. Cook gently for 2 minutes.

▌When the potatoes are cooked, cut a wedge out of each one, and mash the flesh if liked. Spoon the mushroom and hazelnut mixture on top.

TIME: *Preparation takes about 10 minutes. Cooking takes approximately 10 minutes.*

Vegetables

Home-made Herb Mayonnaise

SERVES 4

T*he only way to experience really good mayonnaise is to make your own*

INGREDIENTS

4 large baking potatoes

2 egg yolks

15ml/1tbsp lemon juice

5ml/1tsp English mustard powder

1.75ml/¼ tsp salt

300ml/10fl oz olive oil

1.75ml/¼ tsp freshly ground black pepper

15ml/1tbsp white wine vinegar

15ml/1tbsp each of chopped fresh parsley, basil and oregano

sprigs of parsley to garnish

▌Begin by setting the potatoes to bake in a hot oven as recommended in the introduction.

▌To prepare the mayonnaise, place the egg yolks, lemon juice, mustard powder and salt in a bowl.

▌Beat thoroughly for a couple of minutes until all the ingredients are blended together.

▌Slowly add the olive oil a little at a time, beating well between each addition, until the sauce becomes thick and smooth. This process takes a little time; do not be tempted to rush by adding the oil too quickly as this may cause the mayonnaise to separate. If separation does occur, place a fresh egg yolk in a mixing bowl and gradually beat the mayonnaise into it, and this will correct the consistency.

▌To finish the mayonnaise stir in the pepper, wine vinegar and fresh herbs and chill in the refrigerator.

▌When baked, split the potato across the middle and spoon in the mayonnaise, garnish with a sprig of parsley and serve immediately.

TIME: *Preparation takes about 20 minutes.*

Vegetables

Deep-fried Potato Skins with Salad

SERVES 4

This simple salad preparation mixes together strong flavours to good effect

INGREDIENTS

4 large baking potatoes

1 frisée lettuce

1 bunch of watercress

1 head of chicory

good quality oil for deep frying

FOR THE DRESSING:

30ml/2 tbsp red wine vinegar

75ml/5 tbsp olive oil

10ml/2 tsp Dijon mustard

salt and pepper

▎Begin by setting the potatoes to bake in a hot oven as recommended in the introduction. For this particular recipe it is a good idea to use the largest potatoes you can find.

▎Discard the outer leaves from the lettuce and wash the remainder along with the watercress and chicory in fresh cold water. Drain the leaves well and roughly tear the lettuce and chicory, place in a bowl along with the watercress.

▎To make the dressing place all the ingredients in a screw-top jar and shake vigorously for a few seconds, pour over the salad and gently toss together.

▎When the potatoes are cooked cut them in half and scoop out the majority of the flesh, leaving an even thickness of potato all over.

▎Using sufficient oil to fully submerge the skins, heat to frying temperature and carefully, one at a time, fry each skin until it is crisp and brown. This will take approximately 2 minutes.

▎When cooked allow all the excess oil to run off the skins and leave to cool on absorbent kitchen paper.

▎Sprinkle the skins with a little salt and fill each one with salad, pouring over any dressing that has collected at the bottom of the bowl.

▎Serve immediately with lots of crusty French bread and chilled white wine.

TIME: *Preparation takes about 20 minutes. Cooking takes approximately 5 minutes.*

Vegetables

Carrot & Broad Bean Puffs

SERVES 4

Forget the myths about soufflés, this one is easy to prepare

INGREDIENTS

4 large baking potatoes
225g/8oz fresh carrots
50g/2oz butter
50g/2oz flour
300ml/10floz milk
400g/14oz can of broad beans, drained
75ml/3oz Parmesan cheese, grated
4 eggs, separated
salt
cayenne pepper

▍Begin by setting the potatoes to bake in a hot oven as recommended in the introduction.

▍Peel the carrots and roughly chop, cook in plenty of boiling salted water until soft, then drain thoroughly and put to one side.

▍Melt the butter in a saucepan and add the flour, stir continuously for a couple of minutes, allowing the flour to cook but not colour.

▍Slowly stir in the milk a little at a time until it has all been incorporated and you have a thick, smooth sauce, then remove the pan from the heat.

▍Place the cooked carrot, broad beans, grated cheese and egg yolks in a food processor and blend until smooth. Add this paste to the sauce and beat together well.

▍Season the mixture with a good pinch of salt and cayenne pepper, then pour the mixture into a mixing bowl.

▍When the potatoes are cooked cut them in half and using a spoon, remove the flesh from inside each one leaving a thin lining of potato in each skin. Mash the flesh of two of the potatoes and stir into the sauce. In a clean bowl whisk the egg whites until they form stiff peaks and carefully fold them into the sauce.

▍Arrange the skins on a baking sheet and fill each one two-thirds full with the soufflé mixture.

▍Place in a preheated oven 190°C/375°F/Gas Mark 5 for 20–25 minutes or until firm to the touch. Serve immediately.

TIME: *Preparation takes about 10 minutes. Cooking takes approximately 45 minutes.*

Potato Fillings

Index

anchovies, fresh, in chilli oil 46
aubergines, ratatouille 61
avocados
    and prawns 38
    spicy guacamole 59

bacon
    and broad beans 33
    and cheese 26
    and mushrooms 14
    sausage and egg 20
beans, mixed salad 54
beef
    chilli 19
    Chinese, and green pepper 23
    with coconut sauce 12
broad beans
    and bacon 33
    and carrot puffs 75
broccoli, and ham 18

calamari *see* squid
carrots, and broad bean puffs 75
cashew nuts, with red cabbage 62
cauliflower, sultana cauliflower
    cheese 67
cheese
    Bavarian, and coleslaw 68
    blue, and walnut 65
    cream cheese and spinach
        soufflé 64
    goats', with basil 69
    Gruyère, and bacon 26
    Parmesan, and Parma ham 25
    sultana cauliflower cheese 67
chick peas, curry 68
chicken
    and apricot curry 32
    crunchy chicken 26
    with garlic butter 22
    honey-glazed 15
chilli, beef 19

chillies
    fresh anchovies in chilli oil 46
    spicy guacamole 59
chorizo, and spicy tomato 17
coconut, sauce with beef 12
coleslaw, and Bavarian cheese 68
crab, and prawn 48
cream, and spinach sauce, with
    squid 51
cream cheese, and spinach
    soufflé 64

eggs
    curried with potato 60
    and kipper mash 42
    sausage and bacon 20
    scrambled, with smoked
        salmon 39

goats' cheese, with basil 69
guacamole, spicy 59

haddock, smoked, with
    tomato 36
ham
    and broccoli 18
    Parma, and cheese 25
hazelnuts, and garlicky
    mushrooms 70

kippers, and egg mash 42

lamb, in rosemary gravy 28

leeks, Welsh tatties 56
liver, with red onions 34

mayonnaise
    home-made herb 72
    lime and dill 43
mince, savoury 19
mushrooms
    and bacon 14
    garlicky, with hazelnuts 70
mussels, steamed, with
    parsley 41

onions, with liver 34

peanut butter sauce 27
peppers
    green, with Chinese beef 23
    ratatouille 61
    with tuna 45
pork
    barbecued belly 31
    savoury mince 19
potatoes
    baking 10
    choosing 10
    deep-fried skins with salad 73
    storing 10
    varieties 10
prawns
    and avocado 38
    and crab 48
    king, in mayonnaise 43

ratatouille 61
red cabbage, with cashew nuts 62
salad
    with deep-fried skins 73
    mixed bean 54
salmon
    red, piquant flaked 39
    smoked, and scrambled
        eggs 39
sardines, and tomato hash 46
saté, with peanut sauce 27
sausage
    chorizo and spicy tomato 17
    egg and bacon 20
seafood, and tomato 48
smoked haddock, and tomato 36
smoked salmon, and scrambled
    eggs 39
spinach
    and cream cheese soufflé 64
    and cream sauce, with squid 51
squid, in spinach and cream
    sauce 51
steak
    mini saté and peanut sauce 27
    spice-dusted, with coconut
        sauce 12
tomatoes
    and chorizo sausage 17
    and sardine hash 46
    and seafood 48
    and smoked haddock 36
    tuna, with multi-coloured
        peppers 45

vegetables, spicy curry 57

    walnuts, and blue cheese 65
whitebait, devilled 52